LET'S GO DINOSAUR TRACKING!

by Miriam Schlein ■ pictures by Kate Duke

HarperCollins*Publishers*
JAN 2 7 1992

The illustrator would like to thank Dr. Leo Hickey, Professor of
Geology and Biology at Yale University and Curator of Botany at the
Peabody Museum of Natural History, and Armand Morgan of the
Peabody Public Education Department for their generous donations
of time and information.

Library of Congress Cataloging-in-Publication Data
Schlein, Miriam.
    Let's go dinosaur tracking! / by Miriam Schlein ; pictures by Kate
Duke.
        p.   cm.
    Summary: Explores the many different kinds of tracks dinosaurs left
behind and what they reveal about the dinosaurs themselves.
    ISBN 0-06-025138-7. — ISBN 0-06-025139-5 (lib. bdg.)
    1. Dinosaurs—Juvenile literature.   2. Footprints, Fossil—
Juvenile literature.   3. Paleontology—Juvenile literature.
[1. Dinosaurs.   2. Fossils.   3. Paleontology.]   I. Duke, Kate, ill.
II. Title.
QE862.D5S36   1991   90-39632
567.9'7—dc20   CIP
                                                                  AC

The illustrations in this book were drawn in pen and ink and
painted with watercolors.

LET'S GO DINOSAUR TRACKING!

Put on your boots.

Put on your pith helmet.

And take some water in a canteen.

We're going to do some dinosaur tracking.

Here's the first set of tracks.

Who made them,

and what do they tell us?

We know one thing right away.

Each footprint is 38 inches long.

Whoever made these tracks

sure was big.

And heavy!

Look how deep the footprints are.

We can stand in them.

There's a fish swimming in one!

Who made these giant steps?

More than 100 million years ago
a big sauropod walked by
along a mud flat
by the side of a lagoon.
The feet that made these footprints
carried a 70-foot-long 30-ton body.
No wonder they sank so deep
in the mud!
Sand blew over the mud
and covered the tracks.
In time—millions and millions
of years of time—
the mud turned to stone
and saved this track
to tell us that all those
years ago a sauropod went by here.

9

Look! He wasn't alone.
Here are different tracks—
with three pointy claws.
This is bad news.

These are probably the footprints
of an allosaur—
a meat eater, with big jaws
and sharp, curved teeth.
Spying the sauropod,
the allosaur began running after him.
The sauropod looked like a good
meal to him.

Did he ever catch him?
Or did the sauropod get away?
We don't know.
The tracks lead under a big
limestone cliff.
We can't get to them.
Maybe someday we'll find out
how the story ended.

These chase tracks were discovered
near the town of Glen Rose, Texas, in 1938,
by dinosaur expert Roland Bird.
People around there always thought
they were just big holes in the ground.
But when Bird saw them,
he knew right away they were dino tracks,
probably the tracks of a sauropod.
But what kind?
Because of bones found nearby,
scientists think the tracks
were made by a kind of sauropod
known as a brachiosaurid.

Another time when Roland Bird was in Texas,

someone said to him,

"Say, do you want to see some

elephant tracks?"

Bird went with the man

to a ranch near San Antonio.

Let's take a look at what they saw.

14

There's one problem.
Scientists can analyze rock
to see how old it is.
They could tell that this rock with the tracks
was formed more than 100 million years ago.
There *were* no elephants then!
So—who made these "elephant tracks?"

The truth is, it was another sauropod.
The track looks different from the others
because it's only the front footprints.
Now wait a minute!
Don't tell me the sauropod was doing
some kind of acrobatic balancing act,
walking on his front feet!
What was going on, anyhow?

Here's a clue....

There's also one single sauropod *hind* footprint.

17

Have you ever pushed yourself along
in shallow water, "walking" on your hands
along the bottom, with your
body and feet drifting behind you?

That's what the sauropod was doing—
pushing himself along in water
with his front feet,
leaving these "elephant tracks"
to puzzle us
more than 100 million years later.
He left that one back print
when he was kicking into a turn.
We can see something else.
These prints are not so deep.
That's because his body weight
was being buoyed up by the water.

19

Let's go.

There are more tracks to follow.

Have you got your flashlight ready?

We're going down 400 feet

into a Colorado coal mine.

How can we find dino tracks down here?

There they are—up on the ceiling!
Big, three-toed footprints.
They're 34 inches long
and 34 inches wide.
But how could the dinosaur walk
underground, upside down?

STATES MINE CO.

This is what happened.

About 80 million years ago

a 25-foot-tall hadrosaur came by here.

Sometimes it walked on all fours.

Other times it stood up

on its hind legs

to browse on conifers and palm trees.

When it wanted to move fast,

it ran on its hind legs.

This one was not hanging around, browsing.

The footprints are 15 feet apart.

That shows it was running fast

through the soft peat.

Why?

We can only guess....

Time passed.

The peat hardened to coal,

leaving these tracks

for us to find.

1.

2.

3.

Of course, the hadrosaur was not
walking underground,
or upside down.
What happened was this:
Over millions of years
sand and sediment
settled over the spot
till the footprints were buried
deeper and deeper.
They were not seen again
till the mine was dug.
And he wasn't walking
upside down either.
What we see here is the *bottom*
of the prints.

4.

Get on board.
We're going to France.
Do you have your magnifying glass
and notebook? Good.

Here we are,
in a limestone quarry.

What's this?
Chicken tracks?
What's a chicken doing back
in dinosaur times?

It does look like chicken tracks.

But you're right.

There were no chickens in dinosaur times.

The tracks were made by a chicken-sized
dinosaur named *Compsognathus*.

One hundred forty-five million years ago
this 2-foot-long
6-pound mini-dino
ran along on skinny legs
and birdlike feet.
What was it doing?
Probably chasing a little lizard,
which it ate.
It's one of the smallest dinosaurs
we know of.

Now that we've seen the "chicken tracks,"
it's easy to understand the
mistake that Pliny Moody made.
Pliny was plowing a field on his
father's farm in Massachusetts
when he uncovered a flat piece
of stone with a footprint in it.
It looked like the print of a
pretty big bird—maybe a turkey.
That's what Pliny thought.

Scientists came to look at it.

They agreed with Pliny.

The footprint, they said,

must have been made long ago,

by some big bird.

Well, they were right about "long ago."

But they were wrong about the bird.

The truth is, the stone was 200

million years old. And the print

on it was a dinosaur footprint.

It's easy to understand this mistake.
The year was 1802.
At that time people did not know
there *was* such a thing as a dinosaur.

More people found
"stony bird tracks."
Some prints were really big—20 inches long.
People thought they were made by
giant wading birds, taller than giraffes,
that at one time lived in New England.

Coelephysis

Heterodontosaurus

Dryptosaurus

We know now that these were all
dinosaur tracks.
Lots of different dinosaurs
had birdlike feet.

Dino tracks can give us clues
about how dinosaurs lived—
things we wouldn't know
by just looking at their fossilized bones.
The Glen Rose sauropod track
showed that sauropods walked on land.
Before then, paleontologists
used to think that sauropods had to live in water
because their bodies were too heavy
to be supported by feet.

Different sauropod tracks showed something else—
that these giant plant-eating dinosaurs
often traveled in herds, the way elephants do.
The young ones walked in the middle,
where they were protected.

Tracks of many *Deinonychus*
are found bunched together.
They show that these flesh-eating dinosaurs
probably did their hunting in packs.

Tyrannosaurus tracks show us
that these big flesh-eaters
traveled alone, or in pairs.

We used to think all dinosaurs

were very sluggish and slow.

Dinosaur tracks tell us

this was not really so.

By studying tracks

scientists now have ways to figure out

how fast different dinosaurs could run.

Some, they say, were pretty speedy.

"Ostrich dinosaurs" could probably run

at the rate of 35 miles per hour (mph) or more.

This is not as fast as a race horse (45 mph).

But it's faster than an elephant (22 mph).

Most scientists think that *Tyrannosaurus*
was slow and clumsy.
But some experts now believe it possible
that *Tyrannosaurus* may have been able to
run up to 30 mph—at least for a short distance.

Tracks made in Texas by some therapods
(two-footed flesh-eaters)
showed a running speed of 26 mph.

A hadrosaur track showed
a running speed of 16 mph.

Apatosaurus (a kind of sauropod)
left a slow-speed track—about 2 to 4 mph.
(This is like the walking speed of a human.)
We do not know, though, if this was its top speed.
It may have been walking slowly,
through mud, or just not been in a hurry.

Tyrannosaurus

Ceratosaurus

hadrosaur

Apatosaurus

41

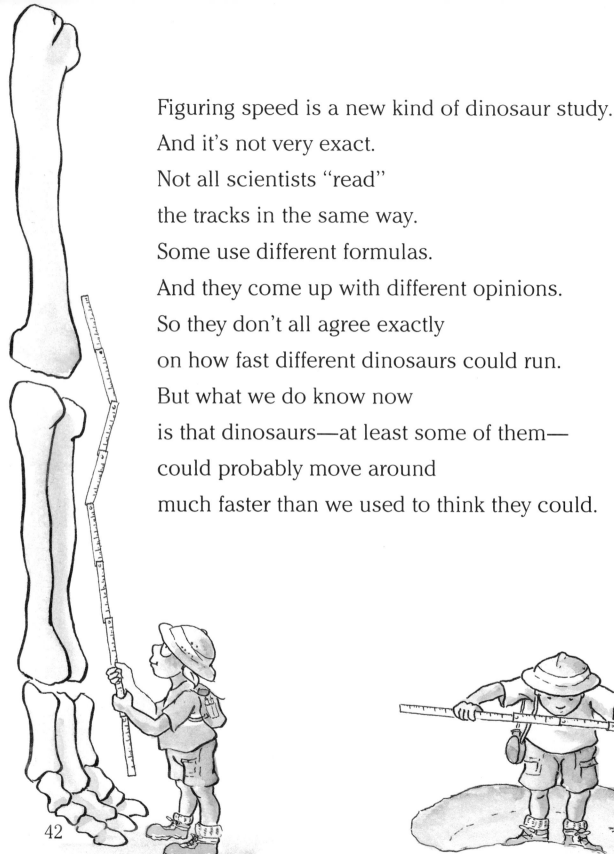

Figuring speed is a new kind of dinosaur study.

And it's not very exact.

Not all scientists "read"

the tracks in the same way.

Some use different formulas.

And they come up with different opinions.

So they don't all agree exactly

on how fast different dinosaurs could run.

But what we do know now

is that dinosaurs—at least some of them—

could probably move around

much faster than we used to think they could.

Some Facts Scientists Use to Figure Dino Speed

1. Length of dinosaur's **stride**. This is the distance from one footstep to the next step of the same foot.

   With animals of the same size, a longer stride shows faster speed.

2. **Hip height**. We get this by measuring the length of the leg bones.

3. **Size of foot**. We get this from the footprint.

4. **Width of track**. Usually, a wide track has been made by a slow walker. A narrow track shows faster speed.

wide track

narrow track

Test your own stride:

1. Find a place where your footprints will show (in damp sand).
2. Walk slowly.
3. Walk faster.
4. Run.
5. Measure the stride of each set of footprints..
6. Which prints show the longest stride? (Running)
    Which prints show the shortest? (Slow walking)

Well, this pith helmet is hot.

My canteen is empty.

My boots are covered with mud.

Let's go home and think about
the things we've learned from
tracking dinosaurs.

Some traveled
in herds.
Some traveled
alone.

A Note about Dinosaur Names

allosaur means "other lizard."

Apatosaurus ("deceptive lizard") is the name now used for the dinosaur we used to call Brontosaurus.

Compsognathus means "pretty jaw."

Deinonychus means "terrible claw," because this dinosaur had sharp, curved five-inch-long claws it used to slash its prey.

hadrosaur means "big lizard." Hadrosaurs are often called "duckbills" because they had flat, wide, ducklike bills.

iguanodont (or **iguanodontid**) means "iguana tooth." (Its teeth resembled those of an iguana.)

ornithopod means "bird-foot." These were dinosaurs whose feet were similar to those of birds.

ostrich dinosaurs were given this name because they were built much like today's ostriches. Their scientific name is *ornithomimid* ("bird imitator").

sauropod means "lizard foot." They were so named because, like lizards, they had five-toed feet. There were many different kinds of sauropods.

theropod means "beast foot." Theropods were two-legged flesh-eating dinosaurs.

Tyrannosaurus means "tyrant lizard"—so named because it was first thought that this powerful flesh-eater with its sawlike teeth was a tyrant to other dinosaurs. (Some scientists now think that probably most of the time what *Tyrannosaurus* ate was carrion—animals that are already dead. So maybe it was not such a "tyrant" after all.)